MW01141411

GRIDIRON GLORY

CELEBRATING OVER 100 YEARS OF
MISSISSIPPI HIGH SCHOOL FOOTBALL

GRIDIRON GLORY

CELEBRATING OVER 100 YEARS OF MISSISSIPPI HIGH SCHOOL FOOTBALL

X.M. FRASCOGNA, JR.
X.M. FRASCOGNA, III
MARTIN FRANK FRASCOGNA

GRIDIRON GLORY: CELEBRATING OVER 100 YEARS OF
MISSISSIPPI HIGH SCHOOL FOOTBALL
Copyright © 2010 by Gridiron Gold, LLC
All Rights Reserved.

Published by the Mississippi Sports Council,
a division of Velocity Sports and Entertainment, Inc.
Post Office Box 16067, Jackson, Mississippi, 39236

Dust cover design, photographs and text layout design by Greg Pevey.
Unless noted otherwise, all photographs in Gridiron Glory are the property of the respective
high schools, the person depicted therein or the Mississippi High School Activities Association.

ISBN: 978-0-9789438-4-4
Printed in the United States of America

First Edition

Without limiting the rights under the copyright reserved above, no part of this publication may be reproduced, stored in or introduced into a retrieval system, or transmitted, in any
form or by any means (electronic, mechanical, photocopying, recording or otherwise), without
the prior written permission of both the copyright owner and the above publisher of this book.

The scanning, uploading and distribution of this book via the Internet or via any other
means without the permission of the publisher is illegal and punishable by law. Please purchase
only authorized electronic editions and do not participate in or encourage electronic piracy of
copyrighted materials. Your support of the authors' rights is appreciated.

Gridiron Glory is dedicated to Dr. Ennis H. Proctor, Executive Director, Mississippi High School Activities Association, and to Dr. Phyfa Eiland, Director of Development, Mississippi High School Activities Association, for their outstanding service as educators and administrators for almost five decades to the high school students of Mississippi. Both Ennis and Phyfa leave a legacy of integrity and honor. Congratulations on a job well done.

ACKNOWLEDGEMENTS

The authors wish to thank all those who submitted photographs from their respective schools and personal archives. A special thanks to our good friend Mark Hinkle, sports photographer extraordinaire, for his submissions to the book along with the contributions of Tim Little, Rives Photography, King Photography, Dr. Joel Butler, Buz Phillips, Ike S. Trotter, Brian Sellers, Darrin Hearndon, Bobby McDuffie, Dr. Joe Moak, Greg Pevey and Malcolm Morehead. The authors are most appreciative of the efforts of Greg Pevey in selecting and arranging the photographs for the book. Finally, a universal thank you to all those who participate every fall in the pageantry of Mississippi high school football. Everyone--coaches, players, fans, bands, cheerleaders, dance squads, teachers and parents--you are all part of Mississippi's *Gridiron Glory*.

X.M. Frascogna, Jr.
X.M. Frascogna, III
Martin F. Frascogna

FOREWORD

In 1905 as Yazoo City played Winona, football began its history in Mississippi. A century later we celebrated that small beginning with thousands of players throughout the state wearing a decal on their helmets hailing a "hundred years of Mississippi football." The sport grew from two small teams to 22,000 players in that period of time, and today Mississippi has one of the highest per capita participation rates in high school football in the nation.

The last century has seen quite a change in the sport, and I've personally seen much of that change since I began playing football in the mid 1950's. I remember the thrill I felt when I moved from the junior varsity leather helmets to the Riddell suspended headgear of the Miami Senior High team, but we've seen changes in all of the equipment from helmets to pads to shoes. The equipment is much safer today-and it needs to be. When I played on the Florida state championship team in 1959, a 185 pound lineman was big. Today 250 to 300 pound linemen are not unusual, and backs and receivers are larger and much faster than they were in my high school years.

I believe football players on the high school and college level exhibit more hard work and courage than in any other sport. I know other sports sacrifice and work hard. However, a 165 pound cornerback must demonstrate tremendous courage as he faces the physical challenge of bringing down a 220 pound hard-driving running back. The only thing that might take as much courage in another sport is a batter standing in the batter's box and facing a pitcher's 100-mile-an-hour fastball. I've always believed that courage comes with confidence. Coaches need to remember this fact when that young football player comes out for the first time and is asked to tackle a larger player. I have seen youngsters shy away initially. However, when some of these same young men gain confidence in themselves and see that they can succeed, they can and do have the courage to tackle that larger player in the game and in life. Some of these shy players end up being the best of our players and the best of citizens; they literally grow into the game.

We've seen other changes in Mississippi football. When I began coaching in 1964, my players were all white. When integration occurred during my Raymond High School season of 69-70 and my Wingfield High School season of 70-71, we brought the talent of our schools together; and Mississippi football rose to a higher level of talent and of competition.

During the forty-seven years I coached, was a school administrator, and served as executive director of the Mississippi High School Activities Association, I saw football evolve from the straight-T formation to the I formation to the wing-T formation to the current spread formation, which uses a more balanced attack between the running game and the passing game. In the 1950's and 1960's, football was 80 percent a running game with very little aerial attack. Today the opposite is true.

Through the years I've also seen the loyal fan base grow increasingly involved, but in some cases they have become overly involved to the point that coaches lose their jobs because of the pressure from the fans. I feel that many of our fans today lose focus of what the priority should be for our high school athletic programs. We know that winning is important-because Americans love winners. However, high school football should be about developing the character of these young men, and our main priority should be teaching them to be better citizens in society. During the years I coached, I was fortunate to have some very good athletes with some being high school All-Americans. I also experienced what it was like to be on the opposite end of the spectrum, where my players were not as physically talented. I was proud of all of my players, and just as proud--if not more so--of those players who gave 100 percent effort yet came up on the losing end.

Football championships in Mississippi have also seen great change. I was one of the coaches who really pushed hard for state championships in Mississippi. When I was involved in the Mississippi Association of Coaches, I served as chair of the football committee. We were successful in changing our system, and today we have state championships in six classifications. The playoffs have created much more interest from our small schools to our large schools with the championships being played at Mississippi Veterans Memorial Stadium the first weekend in December in front of crowds totaling over 40,000 fans. When these young men get the opportunity to play in this large stadium venue, they form lifetime memories. Being a part of any football team on the high school level is something that we hear young and old men talk about for the rest of their lives.

We heard those football reminiscences as coaches and players gathered after the publication of *Gridiron Gold* and *Y'all vs. Us*, books written by X. M. Frascogna and his sons Mike and Marty. With a personal passion for the sport, the Frascogna family has captured the history of Mississippi football through their publications. I thank them for giving me the opportunity to write the foreword for *Gridiron Gold*, the epilogue for *Y'all vs. Us*, and now the foreword for the pictorial of Mississippi football. They have captured the significance of this sport to individuals, communities, and the culture of our state; and they have raised the image of our state through their publications.

I also thank the Mississippi coaches and administrators I've had the opportunity to work with over the last 47 years. They are clearly dedicated and loyal to their responsibility to develop good citizens for the future. The majority of these are Godly people who have used athletics and activities to teach many of life's most important lessons.

As I look at my retirement in 2011, I'm amazed by the changes I've personally seen in Mississippi football and I'm appreciative of the opportunity to be a part of that change. I feel my involvement in athletics in this state has been a blessing to my family and to me, and I'm proud that I've been able to be even a small part of the Mississippi athletic scene for these years. May God bless all of you--and may God continue to bless this great game of football in Mississippi.

Dr. Ennis H. Proctor
Executive Director,
Mississippi High School Activities Associtaion

INTRODUCTION

In 2007 the authors wrote *Gridiron Gold, Inspiring Stories of Legendary Mississippi High School Coaches, Guardians of the Greatest Football Talent in America,* which was the first of three books about the special relationship between Mississippians and the game of football. There are reasons for this phenomenon that can be traced to economic, political, religious, educational and cultural factors that have been forged by generations of Mississippians, resulting in the greatest football talent in America.

While *Gridiron Gold* explores the many aspects that make high school football so unique in Mississippi, its sister book, *Gridiron Glory, Celebrating Over 100 Years of Mississippi High School Football,* tells the same fascinating story in photographs. From the first high school football game in Mississippi in 1905, down through the '20s, '30s, '40s and '50s, photographs of teams, players, coaches, and memorable events like the big Thanksgiving Day battle between McComb and Brookhaven, will rekindle your nostalgia of these times. Many of Mississippi's legendary coaches during the '60s, '70s and '80s are portrayed throughout the book. Beginning in the '90s, the so called "modern era", color photographs bring the action off the pages into the readers out stretched arms.

To fully appreciate the story the photographs in *Gridiron Glory* tell about Mississippi's fabulous gridiron history, readers are encouraged to acquaint themselves with the factors that shape the unique football culture of Mississippi as developed in the predecessor book to *Gridiron Glory,* its older sister, *Gridiron Gold.*

Small Town America

The starting point for an analysis of Mississippi high school football begins with the geography and demographics of the state. Admitted as the 20th state in 1817, Mississippi's boundaries encompass 30,019,840 acres covering 46,906 square miles. The 2000 Census recorded Mississippi's population as 2,844,658, which ranked it as the 31st state in terms of population. By comparison, Mississippi's sister states, Alabama, Louisiana, and Tennessee, have populations of 4,447,100; 4,468,976 and 5,689,283, respectively. For reference purposes, at the top of the population chart are California with 33,871,648; Texas with 20,851,820; and New York with 18,976,457.

As a byproduct of its small population base, Mississippi is made up of a collection of small towns ranging from Jackson, the state's largest city with a population of 177,977, and dropping off to the second largest city of Gulfport with a population of 72,464. (These are preHurricane Katrina numbers.) Out of 112 cities in Mississippi, 75 have populations of fewer than 10,000.

Population demographics play a significant role in the attitude of Mississippians toward their high schools. The local high school teams, especially the football team, become the billboard for the entire community. This billboard is viewed by not only the local community, but by the entire state and, in some instances, the nation.

The Bible Belt

Mississippi is in the middle of the Bible Belt. Neither the Bible nor the belt is spared.

Both are still relied upon in raising children in Mississippi. Both Bible and belt help establish clear boundaries for parents and children. There are rules. Parents expect those rules to be followed in the high schools, too. Failure to follow the rules will result in punishment.

In addition to parents and children benefiting from the structure established by well-defined and enforced rules, there are other beneficiaries--primarily coaches and teachers. Respect for authority is commonplace, especially when it comes to members of athletic teams at high schools in Mississippi. Players listen to and obey their coaches. Otherwise, there are consequences. Oftentimes, the head football coach is the unofficial ultimate authority, primarily because it is the head coach who determines who will take the field on Friday nights in the fall. Failure to follow the rules during the season and during the eight months of off-season training can lead to the embarrassment of standing on the sideline on game day. The head football coach alone determines who will be on the field representing the community on Friday night.

Ministering with a Whistle

Many of the coaches in Mississippi view what they do as a ministry, not a profession.

This mindset has been created by a combination of factors: the state's economic status, its sparse population scattered in small communities, the role the church plays in the lives of most Mississippians and the importance of the football team to each community. At the center of the lives of most of the teenagers playing high school football is their head coach. The many stories of coaches helping their players are heartwarming and truly indicative of the spirit driving these men. It is a motivation well beyond the desire to win football games. Their actions reveal the family concept of the football team. One quickly reaches the conclusion that these men are motivated by a higher principle than fame or fortune. It's not about money or glory; it's all about love for their players. In return, the players see it, feel it, and respect it. The coaches are driven by the respect given them by the players.

One Play Changed Everything

During the '60s and '70s our nation experienced the turmoil of social change, which included integration of the public schools. Mississippi, with the highest percentage of African Americans in the country, was at the forefront of the integration controversy. Ironically, the process of integration in Mississippi was relatively smooth, outside the media hotspots of Ole Miss and Philadelphia (MS). The national media enthusiastically depicted the environment in Mississippi as volatile. Considering this portrayal, and the fact that Mississippi had the highest percentage of African Americans, why was the transition relatively calm? Apart from the reality that the powder keg atmosphere described by the media did not really exist, black and white Mississippians shared a common passion; a passion that superseded racial bias--their love of football, particularly high school football.

At the vanguard of integration in Mississippi were the coaches in the separate school systems. These men and women were the

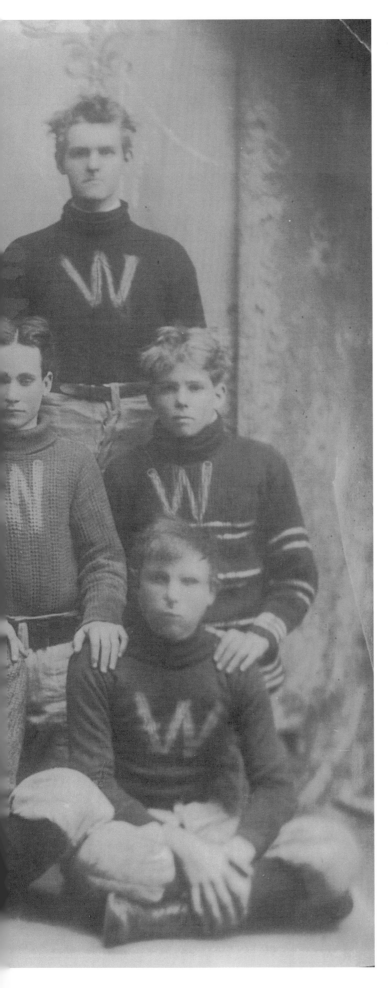

true heroes of social change in Mississippi. Little credit has been given to the coaches who had to overcome so much to protect all the children in the process of combining two separate school systems. Mississippi was truly in a state of flux. The coaches themselves were dramatically affected by new job descriptions, assignments to different schools and, in some instances, reduced compensation. Add to these challenges their own personal opinions regarding the integration process and its effect on their own families. Their task went beyond shaping the attitudes of 40 teenagers on a football team. Those pioneer coaches had to shape the attitudes of entire communities; and they were successful in doing so. The coaches were so successful that they were able to reshape the thinking of an entire state about living in a divided community. The dedication and courage of the coaches during this time of transition led to the smooth combination of the previously separate school systems in Mississippi. By serving in the vanguard of the integration process, Mississippi coaches formed a close bond with their players. That bond has been passed down and still exists today. Mississippi high school teams are like families, and the undisputed head of the family is the head coach.

Blue-Collar Attitude

First, the bad news: Mississippi is a poor state. According to the 2000 Census, Mississippi ranks 50th in terms of personal income per capita. Now, the good news: Mississippians aren't afraid of hard work. From the early days, when farming in Mississippi was the economic engine, hard work was required to survive. Today, farming has been supplemented by timber, shrimping, poultry and oil and gas--all requiring hard manual labor. Mississippians expect to work; and this attitude has been passed down through the generations. A strong work ethic has permeated the attitudes of football coaches, players and fans. The result is that the high school football team symbolizes the community's work ethic. Hard work is not only expected, but demanded, by the community. No high school football team in America will outwork a Mississippi team.

Old-Fashioned Ways

Mississippi is a conservative state. Change comes slowly. In many instances, old-fashioned concepts have withstood the test of time and the influences of modern society. Concepts such as patriotism, religious values, hard work and discipline are still very much alive in Mississippi. For example, the advent of athletes specializing in one sport didn't really gain any traction in Mississippi for two reasons. First, coaches were conservative and resistant to change. And, secondly, the small populations in each community dictated a need for multiple sport participation. Consequently, specialization was delayed in coming to Mississippi high schools. The result was that its football programs remained protected and didn't suffer a drain of talent due to specialization in other sports. Booster club dollars, talented players and fan support remained concentrated on football for a longer time. While many high schools in other states expanded the number of sports offered to its students, Mississippi remained focused on football. The delay in specialization further strengthened football's hold on the community. To this day football is the dominant athletic program at most Mississippi high schools. As an example of the impact of specialization in other states, schools that deemphasized football by adding additional sports were forced to eliminate spring training to accommodate the athletes participating in those sports. As a consequence of Mississippi high schools being slower to adopt specialization, spring training is still intact at all its football-playing schools. According to the Mississippi High School Activities Association, out of 263 high schools in Mississippi, 237 play football. That means 90 percent of Mississippi schools have football programs.

JUCOS

A distinguishing characteristic of Mississippi football is its junior college system (juco), now referred to as community colleges. Presently there are 15 junior colleges in Mississippi, with 14 offering football programs. Other than Mississippi, 17 other states have junior college systems offering football programs. Notably, none of Mississippi's sister states have junior college football programs. The impact of the junior college system on Mississippi football has been significant.

Mississippi junior college football programs provide a large number of high school players an opportunity to continue playing the game. Consequently, a greater number of Mississippi high school players aspire to and go on to play at some college level. This has a twofold result. First, it provides high school players in Mississippi with more opportunities to continue playing the game at the college level. The number of junior college players from Mississippi moving to four-year colleges and eventually to the professional ranks is staggering.

Second, participation in junior college football programs offers men who aspire to enter the coaching ranks more experience as players. They have an additional two years to study the game, experience different coaches' techniques and play at a higher level. Consequently, if and when they elect to coach at the high school level, they possess the advantage of experience over many of their counterparts in other states. This additional experience at the higher level of competition is a distinct asset. The majority of high school football coaches in Mississippi have more collegiate playing experience than their counterparts across the country.

Legacy

Families are the pride of Mississippi. Frequently, many players on a high school football team were preceded by their fathers, grandfathers, uncles, brothers and cousins. Coaches often coach their own sons and sons of former players. Generations of Mississippians are linked by this fraternal connection to their hometown team. As a result, legacies are created. Members of the team want to contribute to the pride of their community's football heritage. It is important to each player because it is important to the community, their families and former players. Each player wants to be a part of the legacy.

Mississippi Pride

Starting in the late 1960s, most of the national media coverage about Mississippi was less than flattering. For the decades following the '60s, Mississippi has been forced to counter many of these negative perceptions created by the media during that tumultuous era of social change.

While most of the nation struggled with the same social issues, Mississippi was the primary target of the media and, as a result, developed somewhat of a complex--a passionate desire to defend the good things associated with Mississippi and disprove the negative portrait of the state. As coaches teach their players, every negative situation provides an opportunity. The key is to always keep playing. The negative images created by the media about Mississippi did just that. Instead of weakening the spirit of Mississippians, it produced an underdog mentality that has been transferred to its high school football teams. Mississippi teams playing across state lines are motivated far beyond normal geographic pride. Intersectional competition is treated as a holy crusade, a defense of the pride of Mississippi against the world. The degrading comments heaped upon Mississippi, even to this day, have only served to boost state pride, particularly pride in all those things Mississippians do best. And one of the things Mississippians are confident they do

well is produce world-class high school football teams. From the smallest high schools in the far reaches of rural Mississippi to their large counterparts in the capital city, all teams, large or small, are competitive. The reputation of Mississippi high school football is protected with a passion not found in other states.

Guardians of the Gold

One of the earliest professional coaches' organizations in the South is the Mississippi Association of Coaches (MAC). Since its inception, the MAC has taken a very active role in conducting and supporting coaching clinics throughout the state. Because of the importance placed on coaching clinics by the association, Mississippi has always been a hotbed for clinics, attracting thousands of coaches from across the country. One of the oldest and most respected clinics, World Gulf Coast Coaching Clinic, founded in 1962 by Coach Lindy Callahan, is now in its 45th year. The MAC's annual clinic has become another learning opportunity for coaches in Mississippi and attracts attendees from outside the state. The coaches in Mississippi have always been eager to expand their knowledge through continuing football education by frequently attending clinics held at colleges and universities in and outside the state.

This insatiable desire to acquire more knowledge about the game has resulted in Mississippi coaches being on the cutting edge of training methods and game strategies. Through these clinics, coaches exchange ideas and concepts about how to improve their own football programs. Because of the friendly atmosphere and willingness to share information, Mississippi has always been one

of the leading producers of football innovation in America.

The football coaches in Mississippi belong to a club, or a fraternity of sorts. There is a strong sense of camaraderie. Maybe with the exception of one Friday night a year, coaches in Mississippi support one another. There is a visible sense of mutual respect among coaches in Mississippi, and in many cases friendship. Members of the coaching fraternity in Mississippi are eager and flattered to share their keys to success with fellow members.

Because of the unusually high number of college football programs in Mississippiespecially in comparison to its small population-collegiate coaching opportunities are numerous. Not only has Mississippi produced a roster of high-profile athletes over the years, it has also served as a breeding ground for legendary college coaches. Famous names such as Johnny Vaught, Pie Vann and Bull Sullivan are just a few who have been recognized nationally. However, once you look deeper--to all the Mississippi junior and senior colleges--the list of famous coaches is endless: Billy Brewer, Buddy Bartling, Harper Davis, Norman Joseph, Sims Cooley, George Sekul, Archie Cooley, Jim Randall, Marino Casem and Dobie Holden, just to name a few. Some of these coaches have attained legendary status, with some reaching mythical proportions. The influence of these famed coaches has been felt in Mississippi, the South and, to a large degree, nationally. Mississippi produces high-quality coaches at all levels of football competition.

To Mississippians, high school football is a necessary obsession. Enjoy the photographs in *Gridiron Glory* depicting this Magnolia mania.

DAD'S DAY and HOMECOMING
ST STANISLAUS COLLEGE
BAY ST LOUIS, MISS.
NOVEMBER 23rd 1924.
STANISLAUS 12   JEFFERSON 0

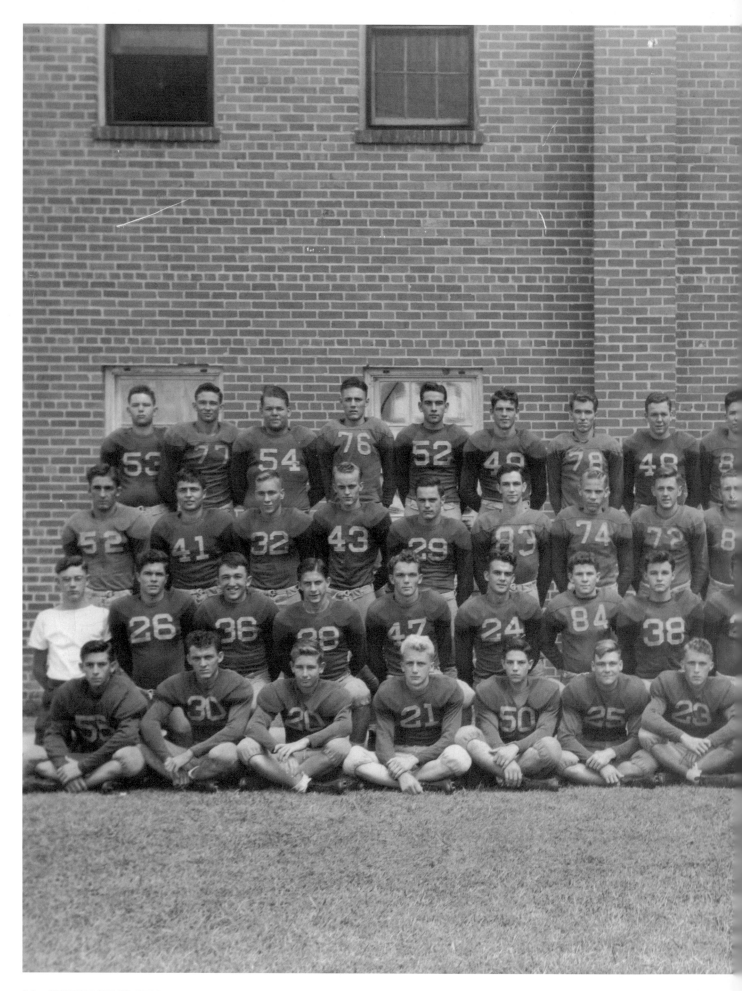

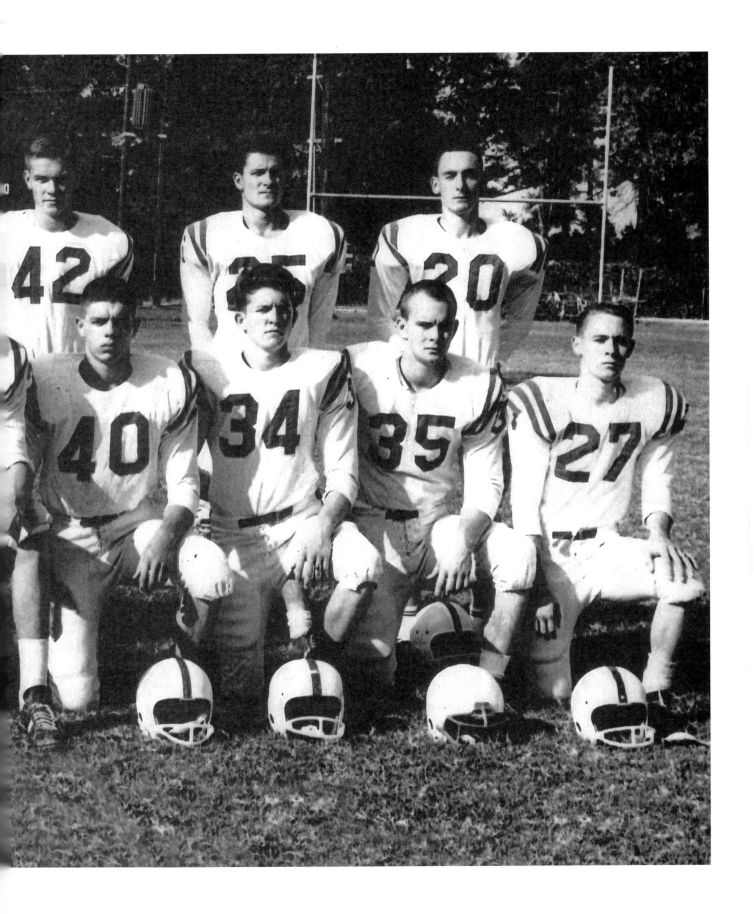

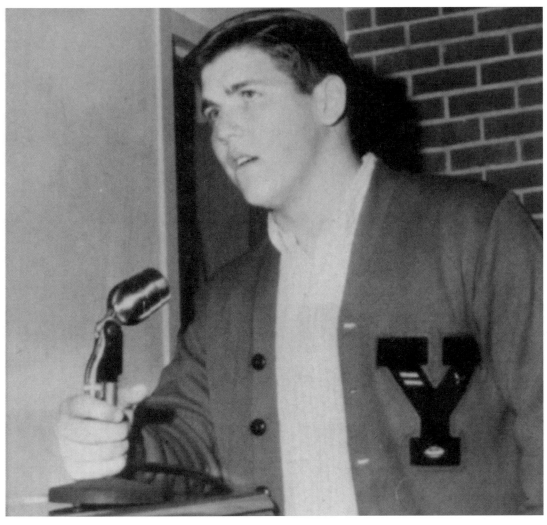

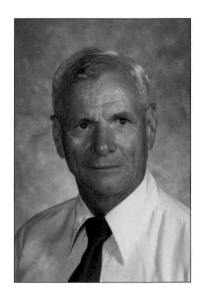

EVERYTHING WE DO HERE IS JUST SO SIMPLE. THE SIMPLER YOU CAN MAKE IT, THE BETTER YOU ARE. IT ALL COMES DOWN TO BLOCKING AND TACKLING. IT'S NOT WHAT YOU KNOW; IT'S WHAT YOU CAN GET THE PLAYERS TO KNOW.

COACH RICKY WOODS
ETHEL | EUPORA | ACKERMAN
SOUTH PANOLA

I'M A CONSERVATIVE COACH THAT BELIEVES IN HARD WORK AND THE CHARACTER OF THE PLAYER.

COACH WILLIS WRIGHT

DREW | CARROLL ACADEMY | SALTILLO
STARKVILLE | GREENVILLE | NETTLETON
SOUTH PANOLA | NORTH DELTA

FOOTBALL IS
THE LAST LINE
OF REAL
DISCIPLINE
THAT WE HAVE
LEFT.

COACH ROBERT MORGAN
WARREN CENTRAL

WITH OVER HALF YOUR ATHLETES COMING FROM SINGLE-PARENT HOMES, THE FOOTBALL PROGRAM BECOMES THE NEW HOME.

COACH MARCELLUS SINGLETON
D'IBERVILLE | ST.JOHNS

Field

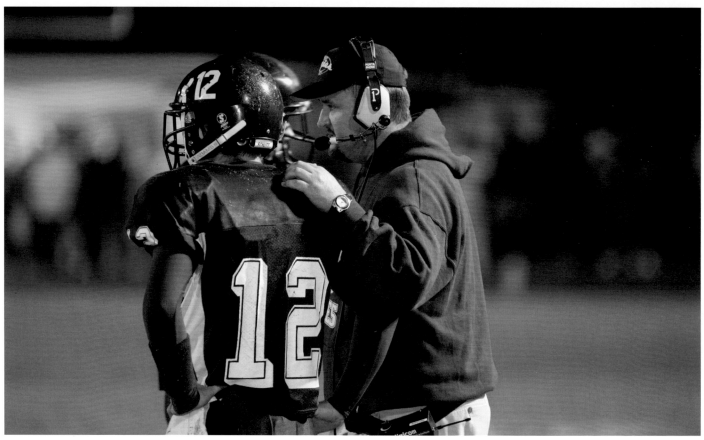

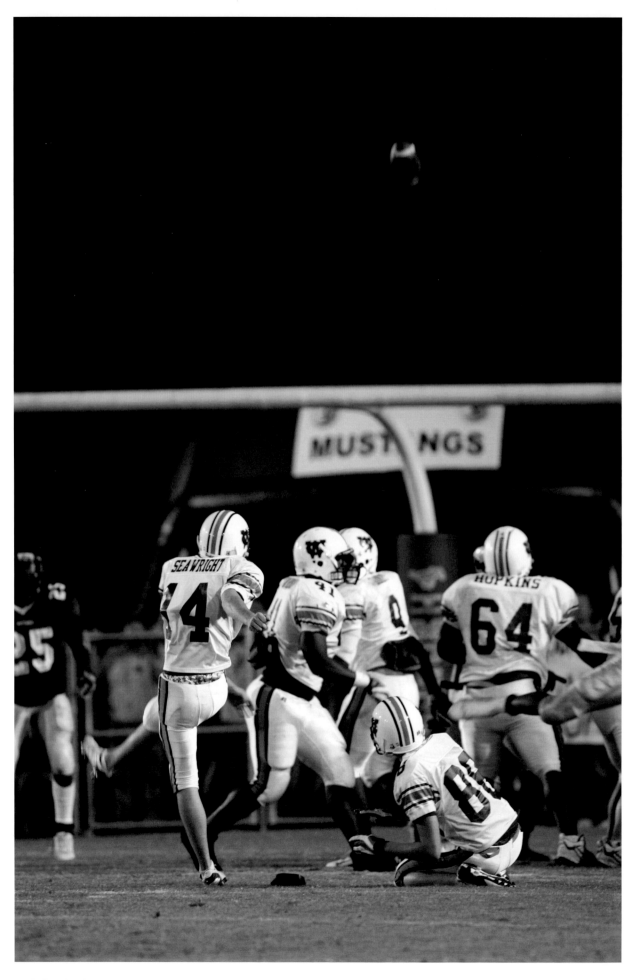

St. Joseph High Rebels

1963

GO LIONS GO!
B. H. S. STUDENT COUNCIL
BURGLUND LIONS
VS.
OAK PARK DRAGONS
(HOMECOMING)
October 28, 1955

EPILOGUE

Over 100 years of pride, passion, and pure obsession for high school football in the state of Mississippi is portrayed in *Gridiron Glory*, a real and lasting tribute to those who helped to create the many traditions that we continue to love and honor today. High school football in Mississippi is akin to religion in the Deep South, with its storied football team dynasties, its intense interstate rivalries, quests for state championships, legendary coaches, and all-time great players who have thrilled their fans, provided bragging rights, and produced some of the most dramatic moments in football history. This book is the ultimate tribute to a tremendous football legacy and lavishly illustrates the players, teams, coaches, games, rivalries, and performances that define decades of football in Mississippi.

However, there is one individual whose name must be included in any story of high school football in Mississippi. Over the last four decades there is one man who has made a tremendous difference and lasting impact upon the sport of high school football in Mississippi--and that individual is Ennis Proctor.

For the past two decades (1991 - 2011) Ennis Proctor has led our schools' student activities and sports to greater and greater heights. His vision, experience, hands-on leadership, and guidance have brought our state into the 21st century as a change in the delivery and consumption of education, activities, and athletics has occurred over the last twenty years. Dr. Proctor has been a catalyst for change, willing to accept new and innovative methods, concepts, and ideas to better sports; and he has been a force in putting into action and promoting the implementation and success of those changes.

His legacy includes many years of dedicated service to this state and will be described as serving with class, charisma, character, integrity, and a genuine love for young people. He consistently demonstrated empathy and understanding with regard to making tough decisions. His has always been an example of Christian leadership--always standing strong for what is right. The MHSAA mission statement talks about fairness and consistency; however, Dr. Proctor has modeled that mission. He has become legendary in his effort to help the student when he can, without regard to criticism or external pressure. Dr. Proctor has influenced so many in a positive way through his constant civility in every situation.

Dr. Proctor has overseen many rule changes and revised regulations as the strategy of playing the game of football evolved from the single-wing to the full-house back backfield, from the power-I to wish-bone and split-back veer option offenses, from the shotgun to the no huddle, one-back to no-back spread today. He has watched as teams line up in the six-two defense, five-four, four-three, and today's three-four defense with numerous secondary coverages, including the popular nickel, bump-and-run, press coverage, cover one, cover two, or cover three and umbrella. He has guaranteed that rules changed as the game changed.

His tenure as MHSAA Executive Director led to improvements in player safety and protection from the revolution of the football uniform, from bright-colored, large-numbered jerseys, new and innovative protective padding to superior equipment, state-of-the-art helmets and shoulder pads. He has moved the sport of football from the dad physician who happened to be at the game to comprehensive safety and medical coverage by qualified medical personnel, team physicians, certified athletic trainers at daily practice and at Friday night games. He has overseen the change in high school football facilities to today's state-of-the-art weight training operations and equipment, off-season strength programs, newly built first class field houses, new stadiums complete with durable all-weather synthetic turf fields.

As we bid farewell to Dr. Proctor, we will insure that the Mississippi High School Activities Association continues to promote the positive values of high school football and will provide the necessary resources to insure its success. We will continue to be on the leading edge of safety and innovative ways to enhance our rules and regulations to improve the game and provide the best for our schools, participants, and fans.

The MHSAA recognizes that "football matters" and understands the life-long lessons and skills that the game teaches those who participate and play under the watchful eyes of our professional coaches, officials, and administrators. Playing the game with honor, respect, and great sportsmanship is an excellent example of civility for us all as high school football brings healthy competition for the youth of our state. This sport unifies communities and brings people together for a common cause, to cheer for their team, and support the young people in their school as they give their all to succeed.

On Friday nights in the fall, the crowds emerge, the bands strike up, and exuberant young men full of confidence take the field. Each of these competitions will be the legacy begun and established by Dr. Ennis Proctor as he raised the national reputation of Mississippi and its athletics. We commit to continue that reputation and to move athletics forward in his honor and for the benefit of the young people of Mississippi.

Don Hinton, Executive Director Designee Mississippi High School Activities Association

Captions

Title Page - Murrah Head Coach Jack Carlisle - circa 1962

Acknowledgements - Governor Haley Barbour accepting the 2006 USA Football Award naming Mississippi America's best high school football state.

Foreword - Dr. Ennis Proctor, Executive Director, Mississippi HIgh School Activities Association - 1959

Introduction - Chuck Trotter, Winona - circa 1905

2-3 - Winona High School's first football team - 1905

4 - Coach Lindy Callahan with his 1957 Gulfport High seniors

5 - Columbus Lee High National Championship Team - 1936

6 - Forest County AHS - 1908

6 - St. Stanislaus High School's first football team - 1916

7 - French Camp - 1920

7 - Kilmichael - 1924

8 - Forest County AHS - 1927

8 - French Camp - 1928

9 - French Camp - 1930

9 - Kilmichael - 1931

10-11 - St. Stanislaus, Dad's Day and Homecoming - 1924

12 - Potts Camp - 1932

12 - St. Stanislaus - 1941

13 - Olive Branch - 1948

13 - Olive Branch - 1926

14-15 - Undefeated McComb Tigers - 1946

16-17 - McComb vs Brookhaven annual Thanksgiving Day game - 1949

18 - Harper Davis #37, Clarksdale Wildcats - 1941

19 - Brookhaven cheerleaders lead the Panthers on the field for the annual Thanksgiving Day game against McComb - circa 1949

19 - McComb vs Brookhaven coin toss - circa 1949

20 - Ken Toler, Sr., Inverness quarterback - 1951

21 - Ken Toler, Jr., Jackson Prep wide receiver - 1976

22-23 - Raymond Rangers - 1964

24 - Walter Suggs, Forest County AHS - circa 1950s

25 - J. E. Loiacano, St. Stanislaus - 1956

26 - Jay Lacoste, Gulfport - 1956

27 - Paul Lacoste, Jackson Prep - 1992

28 - Celebration kiss from Coach Kenneth Bramlett to linebacker, Tony Henderson - 1959

29 - Forest High School, Little Dixie Champs - 1969

29 - Governor Haley Barbour sporting his Yazoo City High letter sweater - circa 1964

30-31 - Provine Rams on the move - circa 1960s

32-33 - Broiler Bowl Champs, Forest - 1959

34 - Murrah Mustang's quarterback, Phil Gibson, receiving instructions from Coach Jack Carlisle

35 - Provine Rams' Coach Hollis Rutter being carried off the field by his players after a Big 8 Conference victory - circa 1960s

36-37 - Coach Bill Raphael instructs a Rebel player during Jackson St. Joseph's shocking 1972 upset of Murrah.

38 - Johnny Mims #12, Vicksburg Gators - 1977

39 - Coach Sammy Dantone demonstrating blocking techniques - circa 1978

40 - L to R: 1st row; Willie Young, Bob Tyler, Howard Willoughby, 2nd row; Scott Samsel, Bobby Hall, Bill Matthews, 3rd row; W.C. Gorden, C.B. Cameron, Bubba Davis

41 - L to R: 1st row; Leslie Peters, John McInnis, Ricky Black, 2nd row; Sammy Dantone, Billy Brewer, Roy Burkett, 3rd row; Kenneth Bramlett, Leslie Pool, Robert Morgan

42 - Coach Ricky Woods

43 - Coach Willis Wright

44 - Coach Robert Morgan

Captions

45 - Coach Marcellus Singleton

46 - Coach Willie Collins with four Provine Rams

47 - Don Hinton, Bay Springs Bulldogs - circa 1972

48-49 - Billboard on I-55 North greeting travelers as they approach the city of Batesville--Home of the South Panola Tigers (Courtesy of Malcolm Morehead)

50-51 - Coach Jim Drewry leads the Booneville Blue Devils on the field

52 - West Jones Mustang player (Courtesy of Darrin Hearndon)

53 - Coach Jim Drewry and the Blue Devil coaching staff

54-55 - Pool Field at Olive Branch High School (Courtesy of Buz Phillips)

56 - Conquistadors of Olive Branch prepare to take the field (Courtesy of Buz Phillips)

56 - Clinton Arrow players and cheerleaders in a smack down with cross-town rival Madison Central (Courtesy of Tim Little)

57 - Y'all vs Us - Tupelo Golden Wave and the Starkville Yellowjackets. (Courtesy of Tim Little)

58 - Jackson Prep's Torrey McAlpin #21 leads Marty Frascogna #20 on a sweep against arch-rival Jackson Academy (Courtesy of Mark Hinkle)

59 - Bay High running back on the move

60 - Blocked kick--Almost!

61 - Bay High running back pulling away from two Irish defenders

62 - Forest County AHS blockers leading the way

62 - Coach Larry Dolan directs his Aggie quarterback

63 - Hear come the Pearl Pirates.

63 - Ray Rogers, Pearl High School's first quarterback, leads the Pirates on the field.

64 - Clarksdale's Eric Houston protects a wet football (Courtesy of Rives Photography)

64 - Clarksdale kicker and holder playing in the rain (Courtesy of Rives Photography)

65 - South Panola's Issac Cross (#99) gets up in the face of Petal lineman Garrett Watts (#62) (Courtesy Bobby McDuffie)

66-67 - Pearl Pirate defense attacking a Brandon Bulldog running back

68 - Clarksdale's Myles Malone making the tackle on Southeast Lauderdale ball carrier (Courtesy Rives Photography)

69 - Clarksdale defense buries running back (Courtesy Rives Photography)

70 - Pearl quarterback unloading a pass to his tight end

71 - South Panola stands at the 2009 State 6A Championship Game

71 - South Panola players celebrating the Tigers' victory in the 2009 State 6A Championship

72-73 - A moment of reflection at Jackson Academy Raider Field (Courtesy of Mark Hinkle)

74-75 - West Point players enjoy the mud and the win. (Courtesy of Brian Sellers)

76 - Statue honoring Coach Sherrod Shaw at Jackson Academy's Raider Field (Courtesy of Mark Hinkle)

77 - Statue of Walter Payton at Payton Field, Columbia High School

78 - South Panola player celebrates his team's 2009 State Championship victory in the snow

79 - New Hope's Jeremy Wells leaves Saltillo defender in the mud (Courtesy of Dr. Joel Butler)

80 - Coach Dan Davis giving instructions to Jerious Norwood

81 - Tylertown Chiefs picking up yardage

81 - Tylertown completes a 15-0 championship season in 2009

82 - St. Stanislaus quarterback Dylan Favre launches a pass against Lafayette during the 2009 State 3A Championship

83 - Brookhaven's Jimmy Johns on the loose

84 - Wayne County War Eagle's kicker splits the uprights (Courtesy of Darrin Hearndon)

Captions

85 - Booneville's Blue Devil draws up the famous 48-Sweep

86 - The joy of winning at Warren Central

87 - Hattiesburg Tigers ham it up for the camera

87 - Petal High School - 2008 team *(Courtesy of King Photography)*

88-89 - West Jones and Wayne County battle lines *(Courtesy of Darrin Hearndon)*

90-91 - Jackson Academy Raiders take the field *(Courtesy of Mark Hinkle)*

92 - West Jones Mustangs celebrate a big win *(Courtesy of Darrin Hearndon)*

93 - Coach Alonzo Stevens gets a victory shower from his Vicksburg Gator players

94-95 - The coin toss at West Jones Mustang Stadium *(Courtesy of Darrin Hearndon)*

96 - The Granddaddy rivalry - Gulfport vs Biloxi *(Courtesy of Tim Little)*

97 - Coach Scott Pierson huddles with his West Jones players during a game *(Courtesy of Darrin Hearndon)*

98 - Coach Mike Justice on the Gulfport sideline

99 - Top: Ocean Springs quarterback, Garret Somers, gets hammered by Tylertown defenders *(Courtesy Bobby McDuffie)*

99 - Botton left: Oak Grove quarterback, James McMahon *(Courtesy Bobby McDuffie)*

99 - Bottom right: Ocean Springs running back, Dwayne Cherry, avoids a Hattiesburg defender *(Courtesy Bobby McDuffie)*

100-101 - West Jones player celebrates *(Courtesy of Darrin Hearndon)*

102 - Gridiron joy at Warren Central

103 - Coach Jim Drewry and his assistant coach, Edna Drewry

104-105 - The pride of South Panola - State Championship Footballs

106-107 - Neighborhood rivals Jackson Academy and Jackson Prep *(Courtesy of Mark Hinkle)*

108-109 - Booneville Blue Devils and Baldwyn Bearcats in a stare down *(Courtesy of Tim Little)*

110 - St. Joseph Rebels game program - 1963

111 - Burglund Lions and Oak Park Dragons game program - 1955

112 - Madison Central Jaquars take the field

112 - D'Iberville quaterback, Greyson Chambless *(Courtesy Bobby McDuffie)*

113 - Clinton's Coach Scott Brown and Madison Central's Coach Bobby Hall meet prior to kick-off

113 - Clinton ball carrier trying to break away from defenders

114-115 - Olive Branch Conquistadors at practice - *note scoreboard (Y'all vs Us)

116 - Yazoo County Panther, Kaleb Eulls, became a hero when he subdued a girl with a gun who threatened the children on a school bus.

117 - Top left: Harrison Central's QB, Aerion Williams evades Ocean Springs defenders; Top right: Ocean Springs running back, Eddie Szigeti speeds past Biloxi;
Bottom: Ocean Springs' Alan Howze *(Courtesy of Bobby McDuffie)*

118 - Top left: Biloxi quarterback, Hawton Buchanan
Top right: Moss Point's Quayshaun Williams
Bottom: Ocean Springs' Joseph Morrow

119 - Top: Brookhaven Academy students celebrate the start of a new football season with a parade. *(Courtesy of Dr. Joe Moak)*
Bottom: Parklane Pioneers capturing a Brookhaven Academy Cougar running back. *(Courtesy of Dr. Joe Moak)*

120 - Pearl QB, Davontae Nichols being interviewed by Russ Robinson after their victory over arch rival Brandon. The game was part of Cellular South's Y'all vs. Us broadcast. *((Courtesy of Mississippi Sports Magazine)*

121 - The authors shown with their collection of high school football helmets from across the state of Mississippi. L-R: Marty Frascogna, Mike Frascogna, Mike Frascogna, III *(Courtesy of Mississippi Sports Magazine)*